If the World Were a Quilt

If the World Were a Quilt

Poems by

Charles K. Carter

© 2023 Charles K. Carter. All rights reserved.
This material may not be reproduced in any form, published,
reprinted, recorded, performed, broadcast,
rewritten or redistributed without
the explicit permission of Charles K. Carter.
All such actions are strictly prohibited by law.

Cover art: *jettison* by Claire Quelle
Author photo by Brandon Carter
Cover design by Shay Culligan

ISBN: 978-1-63980-421-4

Kelsay Books
502 South 1040 East, A-119
American Fork, Utah 84003
Kelsaybooks.com

Acknowledgments

Thank you to these literary journals who originally published versions of the following poems, sometimes with different titles:

Active Muse: "Mother"
Beyond Words: "The Art of Leaving"
Dodging the Rain: "Father," "Tribe"
Fevers of the Mind: "Birthright," "Sunflower Meditations"
Ink Pantry: "Splinters"
Limp Wrist: "Baptism," "Survival of the Fittest"
Marias at Sampaguitas: "Wind"
The Mark Literary Review: "Earth"
Nymphs: "Fire"
Paddler Press: "After All This Pressure"
Prismatica Magazine: "The Art of Blending In"
Resurrection Magazine: "Under the Sea"
Sledgehammer Literary Journal: "Caught"
Wine Cellar Press: "Swallowed"

"Cat & Mouse Game" first appeared in Charles K. Carter's chapbook *Chasing Sunshine,* published by Lazy Adventurer Publishing.

"Blue," "Higher Life Form," "Searching," "Water," and "Weather" first appeared in Charles K. Carter's chapbook *Splinters,* published by Kelsay Books.

Thank you, Brandon Carter, for being my love and for always being my sounding board!

Special thanks to Aurora Bones for the profound workshops.

Claire Quelle, thank you for sharing your art.

Sammi Stange, thank you for being a friend.

Contents

If the World Were a Quilt												13

I.

Man Sews His Fears to the Feathers of a
   Predatory Bird												17
From the Cold												18
Birthright												19
Impermanence												20
Pondering the News												21
Cute												22
Cat & Mouse Game												23
This Island												24
Artificial Light												25
The Earth Stood Still												26
Halved												27
A Single Mitochondrion												28
Another Poem to the Moon												29
Call of the Wild												30

II.

The Swamp Witch (Death Wish)												33
Shadows												34
Higher Life Form												35
Wind												36
Splinters												37
Mother												38
Root Ball												39
Transforming												40
The Art of Leaving												41

III.

Desert Flower	45
The Art of Blending In	46
Filicide	47
Weather	48
Branches	49
Forgiveness	50
Baptism	51
Blue	52
Sunflower Meditations	53
After All This Pressure	54
Survival of the Fittest	55

IV.

Splayed	59
Under the Sea	60
Tribe	62
Searching	63
Father	64
Fireside Wisdom	65
Fire	66
Caught	67
Secrets	68
Animal Funerals	69
Earth	70
Water	71
Venom	72
Swallowed	73

"Remember the plants, trees, animal life
who all have their tribes, their families, their histories, too.
Talk to them, listen to them. They are alive poems."
—Joy Harjo

If the World Were a Quilt

If the world were a quilt, it would be decorated in an array of colors. The reds of lava and oranges of fire's blaze. Yellows of tropical birds. The green grasses. Blue whales. Violets. Shades of all people found there. Shades of the seas. The shades in the patches of forests and jungles and swamps, mountains and sandy desert terrains. The patterns of cheetahs and orcas, fox and rattlesnakes. The brightness of a summer dandelion. Darkness of the deepest cave. Its contrasts of beauty abound.

If the world were a quilt and we could see all of its colors laid out and patched together with the love of Mother Nature's gentle stitching, with the loving act of Creation, would we learn to respect it? Would we wrap it around ourselves and allow ourselves to become one with its warmth, with its softness? If the world were a quilt, would we protect it? Or would we destroy it, ripping the seams and pulling it apart thread-by-thread, throwing its tattered remains to the curbside of the Milky Way, ignoring all of its colors, all of its beauty, all of its joy? If the world were a quilt, would it remedy our loneliness? Would we find a way to call this place home?

I.

Man Sews His Fears to the Feathers of a Predatory Bird

I am a hawk,
flying above it all,
seeing all the congregations of beings below:

>productive ants building hills and tunnels,
>bee colonies letting sweetness into the atmosphere,
>flocks of smaller birds migrating in sharp formations,
>humans making love under the stars . . .

but where is my community?

Sometimes I can't stand to see the joy in others,
that they can belong when I do not belong to anyone.
I do not belong to anything but cold nights and biting winds

so I will fly

>up
>up
>up
>up
>up

until I am free-floating in outer space,
suffocating on craving.

From the Cold

I remember walking to school as a kid,
in the biting wind chill that comes to Iowa every January.
I remember turning to face every car that drove by,
quietly hoping for the warmth, kindness, and love
of a total stranger—someone to rescue me from the cold.

As I make it through another day,
imparting the wisdom of critical thinking to the next generation,
as I go through housework and hygiene routines,
I keep checking Tinder for the warmth, kindness, and love
of a total stranger—someone to rescue my heart from this cold.

Birthright

My father is the fly that circles around dead and already digested things, drinking his diet of decay, dreaming of nothing grander than this fly-by dive, thriving on destruction. Eventually, he developed into what he consumes: a diminished fraction of what he once was, a dim decaying shell of a bug buzzing circles around his deformed body's demolition.

I am a product of reproduction. I am a fly because my father was but I have a fondness for the sweeter things. I find fulfillment on ripened fruit. The pulpy pit of a peach pulls me away from the puzzling predicament of my fly-status birthright. I may be from the Diptera order but I will paint these wings—hope for a butterfly's beauty or a dragonfly's grace.

Impermanence

Dancing butterflies
hit windshields—beauty never
lasts in this dark world.

Pondering the News

I saw in the news
that a humpback whale guarded a diver
when a shark appeared.

And I
wonder how animals see
any good in us.

Cute

You look me in my sea-colored eyes,
give me a cockeyed smirk, and tell me I'm cute
but you find bats cute and locusts and spiders too.

Excuse me for not taking your words as a compliment.

Cat & Mouse Game

You found the courage to speak up first, winning our little game
of give and take, of lie and break, our little cat and mouse game.

Which cat would dare bring up the other's infidelities first?
Who so foolish to let the spool of thread slip and lose the game?

We finally chose to "open things up"—just a little bit.
"We can talk to others," you meowed. "That's *all*." Begin

the game: of hiding desires, of setting traps under couches
waiting for some mouse to fall prey, to play in our game,

to lie there restrained, mouths watering for a treat, pump 'n dump.
"We should play with others," you said. A little hump in the game.

But that wasn't enough warm milk or catnip to fulfill you,
you were addicted to cat and mouse, addicted to the game

but this cat lost out, lost out and traded one of his nine lives
to be rid of these fleas and worms, to forfeit your stupid game.

This Island

And you can't help but fall
for the attention from a total stranger,

giddy smiles and fiery eyes
flirting from across a twenty-four-hour diner,

the potential of love
bubbling up, warming your insides.

And you can't help but fall
a little deeper into that pit in your chest,

the pit of hot lava
creating an island of love inside of you.

How do you carry around this mass?

Artificial Light

I wanted inside of you.
I wanted you.
I wanted to be one with your glow.
I was drawn to you not because you were damaged goods
but because you had done so much to heal yourself.
I wanted to snuggle with you on the couch
and eat junk food and learn all of your secrets.
I wanted to talk about how you weathered the storms of
withdrawal.
I wanted to know how you mustered the courage to erase the past
and start again.
I wanted to know what gets you through lonely meals, lonely
holidays, lonely nights.
I wanted to know how therapy worked for you.
I wanted to compare coming out stories and battle scars.
I wanted to know which Britney song served as an escape for you.
I was drawn to your radiant light.
You drew me in;
hypnotized by your flame,
my wings were singed, scarred, and tattered.
I was violently descending,
becoming a worm
doomed to crawl this earth.
I was left broken.
I was left grounded, wanting you.

The Earth Stood Still

When he kissed me good
night on our first date, I did
not know that one day soon he would
stop the sun from shining
or the bees from buzzing—
that all things blessed would be lost
in his black hole mouth.

Halved

Like an earthworm,
you split me in two.

Part of me
crawled after you

and part of me remains,
waiting to regain

the strength to begin again.

A Single Mitochondrion

A reiki healer once told me that a single mitochondrion
from a single cell has enough energy to power all
of New York City for seven days.

You have strength enough in one cell
to overcome your midday lull, to fight through illness,
to reach the finishing line of a race.

But what happens when a cluster of cells is hung up
on a man you should know better than to hold out hope for?
Where does this energy go?

Does it spill out lovesick loneliness?

Another Poem to the Moon

I write poems to
the moon, hoping she listens,
hoping that maybe

she will love me back.
Speak to me, oh-so-full moon,
constant satellite

pulling the tidal
waves of this sorrowful mind:
fill me up with light.

Call of the Wild

As I sat in my solitude
by the fire's glow,
a strange familiarity began to grow.

A wolf stood staring into the mighty flame.
And when she ran off,
I swear I heard her calling out my name.

II.

The Swamp Witch (Death Wish)

The swamp witch is calling me,
lulling me with her music—
her sweet bird song, her cricket chirps,
and frog croaks.

The swamp witch is calling me,
crying out for my body—
luring me
like ancient Greek sailors to the sirens.

The swamp witch is calling me,
looking to consume all of me
and I go—
oh so willingly.

The alligators can suck any remaining meat off my bones.

Shadows

She runs through the woods
—shadows of the tall trees do
engulf her spirit.

Higher Life Form

Humans like to think they are
the highest form of being
in their fleshy wrappers, meat
centers, and their unquenched taste
for destruction. In their few
decades, they stir no magic,
only chaos.

Trees are the highest form of
rebirth. To be reborn a
tree is to be strong, giving,
resistant to change—to sit
and observe the world's beauty
for hundreds of years in great
peace, in stillness.

Wind

Heed the power and the warning of the mother winds:
She has looked upon man

and carried the seductive songs of sirens to their ears,
false hope for the longing-to-be-touched, lonely traveler.

She has curated twisters across the Midwest, tropical hurricanes
carrying lucky pennies, Chihuahuas, and lost hope across this
earth.

She has blown out their light, leaving them in great darkness,
forcing them to face their fears, their regrets, their inner demons.

Men run for safety not knowing that she has power
to blow them out of existence in seconds, snuffing their inner light.

Heed the power and the warning of the mother winds:
She sees all—she knows our history and won't let us repeat it
again.

Splinters

I have found solace in this fluid state, this comforting womb,
this escape from the reality of mankind's mania,
drawn to the water's stillness, its silence, to its blue

but the waves have torn off this false merman tale
and spat me out saltily to the sands above
bidding me no mercy, no protection as the ancient whale

waves a gentle goodbye—I bring my wet, wrinkled fingertips
to brush away these ocean-like teardrops. I pluck
away the barnacles like scabs that have to be compulsively picked

off like a fish being scaled, flaked
until it is merely flesh to be devoured.
I stand vulnerable; human, naked, exposed, scoured.

I am no longer welcome to live in a world
where there is only peace.
I step out of the water and find footing on solid ground,

gravity weighing heavy on these shoulders
taking in the sights of the green earth and the sky's musical sounds
channeling the mighty thunder of the gods to stand tall.

I fear the wind will whisk me away to mere particles of dust
as the hurricane makes slivers of a small, wooden fishing boat.

I would rather be splintered in the sea.

Mother

The circles under her eyes are dark,
hair is shiny, shoulders slouched.
The soles of her shoes are as worn as her weathered face,
taking my tiny fingers in hand,
she gently leads me across the desert.

Tired from walking,
she has a spirit that flies higher than the vultures.
She finds a way to smile through the burning, blinding sun,
to smile through scalding sands
and dirty water that remains in the canteen.

The gods created her
with the strength of the canyons, holding up the sky.
The gods created her with a capacity to love
greater than all water the oceans can hold,
greater than all the rain the clouds can cry.

This is mother. This is Mother.

Root Ball

Plant a root ball
so that it may spread its wings and reach for the sky,
or at least wiggle its fingers in the nourishing soil.

To remain twisted in a ball of self
is to slowly die alone,
unbloomed.

Transforming

There are all of these theories about how we are connected,
that energy is never created nor destroyed,
it just passes on from one form to another,

that a kind word can spark invention,
as the nutrient-rich Saharan sands are swept away across the
Atlantic, taming hurricanes and feeding the forests of the Amazon,

and I wonder what form our love will take when it's over?

The Art of Leaving

When I left him, I
made sure to water him and
tilt him to the sun.

When he left me, he
dug up my roots, trampled me.
He left me wilted.

But I will survive, will
untangle myself, find
holy ground again.

III.

Desert Flower

He was always poking her with cactus needles
and calling it love.

She pretended to be a desert porcupine,
always realigning herself to receive his touch.

He was always crying rushing rivers,
begging for her to soothe his bruised ego once again.

She was a desert octopus,
always hiding out from his rain.

He was always a snake's rhythmic rattle,
hypnotizing her child-like needs.

She was a desert mouse,
trusting the rattle more than the rustling grass.

He was always slipping away like sand,
disappearing into a mirage for days on end.

She treats heartache with aloe vera as if it were a burn,
hoping he will return to her once again

even though she blooms better without him.

The Art of Blending In

There was once a young woman
who was more of a chameleon
than a woman.
Anytime she wanted,
she could slip into someone else's body,
blend herself in their patterns,
disguise herself in their colors.

She could morph into her mother's mulberry lipstick
and call herself out of school.
She could morph into her frenemy
and seek revenge, red splatter on frayed white pants.
She could morph into Grandma's bottled bronze tan
to buy beer and Marlboro menthols.

She could morph out of her own blues
into warmer colors and warmer blood
none of those colors her own.

There was once a woman
who was more of a chameleon
than a woman.
Anytime she wanted
company
she would slip into her brother's skin,
find a woman with a short skirt and white teeth,
to slip into her,
safe for a second.

Filicide

Sometimes,
there are so many roles she has to play:
nurturer, feeder, protector, teacher, healer.
It is exhausting to be everything for another.
It is easy to lose oneself in altruism.
It is easy to lose oneself in obligation.

Sometimes,
the world is not ready for the next generation:
the aged are stuck in a rut, repeating the past over and over,
a cycle of despair they are not ready to let go of.
It is easy to see when one is not welcome.
It is easy to see when one's light is not wanted.

I understand why Mamma Rabbit devours her young.

Weather

Anger is the clouds
rolling through my morning tea.
I keep on sipping.

Branches

Grandpa drank a little too much nectar
of the gods and then grabbed a stick or a
leather belt to whip his own children
into grand groveling submission.

Dad didn't hit too much and he didn't
drink but he beat us with his bellowing
voice, belittled us until those words
appeared on the trunks of my thighs.

I will never become an abusive
father because I cut off all of the
limbs. I cut it down to a stump, counted
the rings, traced them with my thumb and

then lit what remained on fire.

Forgiveness

Gray whales were prime prey, hunted to near extinction.
They were coined *devil fish* for fiercely fighting back
when their young were harpooned,
all too familiar with the violence
in a human's heart.

Now that the hunting has ended,
these same sentient creatures willingly approach
whale-watching boats in Bahía de Magdalena,
mothers with harpoon-inflicted scars lift their calves up,
seeking the love
in a human's touch.

Baptism

Freedom
is running
naked
into the cool California waters
hand-in-hand
with the one you love.

Blue

When I meditate
I find myself floating—a
light feather down

a clear creek lined with
smooth river rock flying by
a fruitful green tree

over a red clay
bluff and into the deep
blue sea—all around

me is nothing but
blue refracting rays of light
from the world above

the blue silence
a womb in its comfort and
its serenity

it's always quiet
at first stuck in the blue but
then comes the eye of

god with her whalesong
guardian of deep keeping
me in light—in peace.

Sunflower Meditations

I want to be like
a sunflower: to be young and to follow
the sun's glow, to be old and

continue growing
tall even as death knocks on
its door, to keep its

head up even as
it witnesses the loss of
the other life, keep

climbing high as if
attempting to reach the sun's
sacred salvation.

After All This Pressure

Dinosaurs died out
but after millions of years
of decomposing

and earthly pressure,
they adventure on—fueling
lifesaving back-up

power sources for
respirators and cell phones,
fueling fun summer

road trips down the west
coast's windy highways, and now
fossil-fueled jet planes

let the ferocious
six-ton tyrannosaurus
rex fly through the clouds.

Survival of the Fittest

Tardigrades can handle
decades in arctic ice
but I can't seem to handle
seeing his name on his un-forwarded mail.

Tardigrades can endure
an active volcano's red lava
but I can't seem to endure
his face showing up on Tinder.

Tardigrades can manage
floating in outer space
but I can't seem to manage
washing the sheets—
they still smell like him.

IV.

Splayed

Write me into a poem, he said;
so I turned
him into ocean spray
on red clay bluff at dawn:
merman crying for escape.

Under the Sea

I.

I want to be where the mermaids are

down where it's better,
down where there's harmony,
where they love all the species of the seas.

down where it's better,
down where sharks are sharks
and not men in suits disguising their lust for blood.

down where it's better,
down where mankind's iron fist
isn't there to grip at the soil or my fragile heart.

II.

My youngest dog is
like Flounder, a loveable
goof following me,

warily wading
behind me as I search for
a scale-bottomed man,

a charming prince to
protect me from the monsters
that walk on this earth.

III.

Disney changed the ending.

In the original story,
the mermaid realizes being human isn't being happy
so she tosses herself, in human-form, off a ship—
in death trying to make her way back home,
diving into the stormy waters, dissolving to sea foam.

IV.

Did you know that Hans Christian Andersen
wrote *The Little Mermaid* as a love letter to another man?
Loving a man in the nineteenth century
was like a fish loving a man.
It would never work.

Sometimes being a man loving another man feels like that in the twenty-first century too.

Tribe

The lion hunts those who fall from the herd.
Tribe does the same, carefully picks its prey.
She's a witch. An adulterer. Slut. Whore.
He's a communist. Fag. A terrorist.
Fear immigrants, natives, the different.
Feed them to the lions. Grab your pitchfork.
Tie her to the stake. Light her up in flames.
No more screams, not a single peep or sound.
Watch Lady Liberty burn to the ground.

Searching

The water drips off
the kayak's white oar, searching
for its way back home.

Father

There is a crow's nest outside my window.
I watch the father crow guard his little one
while the mother goes out for food.

There is a crow's nest outside my window.
I watch the father crow teach the little one
to squawk and flap his downy wings.

There is a crow's nest outside my window.
I step out on the branch over abandoned nest,
I spread my arms and try to fly.

There was a crow's nest outside my window.
I wanted to be his child, his little hatchling.
I wanted to make someone proud.

Fireside Wisdom

I hate rabbits. I hate rabbits. I hate rabbits.

He always swore saying it three times
would drive the smoke away

but he was the fire always burning
on display for me,
not on love or passion
but on unfiltered rage.

And I warned him three times
before he took it too far.

His diminishing smoke turns away from me now,
bowing before my power.

I hate rabbits. I hate rabbits. I hate rabbits.

Fire

Fire is in man's hands.
He can use it as a tool:
the warmth of a fireplace, lighting of a gas grill
—warding off disease.
But man is not responsible for his gift. For he is selfish.
He uses his tools not just for good. But for evil.
He torches the towers of those he does not understand.
He burns the flesh of those who do not agree with him:
lit tires stuck burning the flesh of his enemy's meaty midsections
upwards and outwards
until all that is left
are ruins.

Fire is in Mother Nature's almighty hands.
She holds the true power:
to ignite with lightning,
to burn their houses and their white picket fences,
to burn their histories: their holy books and photographs.
She has the power to destroy
but with her great love,
new life forms
—a dandelion rises
from the ash.

Caught

They say there are trace amounts of antidepressants
in almost all of the lakes and rivers,

not from people flushing pills down the toilet
but from what remains in our waste

and I wonder if the fish are finding more balance in their lives,
if the fish are feeling any happier

or if they are uncomfortably numb, left living in a daze,
swimming directly into the fisherman's net

because that's how I feel.

Secrets

About two blocks down the street from our house,
headed towards the parks by the lake,
I got used to arguing with him and
always having to distract our yippy Shih tzu
from the beautiful old golden retriever
sitting on her porch.
She had earned her relaxation.
She had the secrets of old age.
She had the secrets of life.
She had the secrets of love.

One day she was gone.
A quiet grief overwhelmed me.
I wanted to speak to her,
to know her wisdom.
I wanted her to take my paw and tell me my fortune:
would he ever love me in the way I loved him?

Animal Funerals

I have attended many animal funerals.
I don't remember this,
but I was told while I was in the first grade,
when my grandma's old collie died,
I rode in the backseat with the dog's body covered by a blanket.
When my grandpa turned a corner too fast and the blanket slipped,
I declared that Jessie would be cold
so I slid off my booster seat to cover her up again.
My grandma lost it.

I have attended many animal funerals.
I have raised a toast in memory of Sgt. Fishy,
a dead fish near the shore of a pond.
I have comforted a friend after she accidentally
hit a cat on the four-lane highway.
I have gasped in awe at a purposefully destroyed goose nest.
I have cried in anger upon finding
a den of fresh otter pups stomped in.

I have attended many animal funerals
but I have never had to mourn the loss of a companion animal,
a dog who would curl up on the bath mat
while I read for hours in the tub,
a friend who is a part of my every day,
who fills my cup with love when it is running empty,
licking away my tears.
How will I fair when that day comes?
How will I not completely crumble
when I find her hair under the couch cushion after she's gone?

Earth

The creature walks barefoot on this earth,
feeling a connection to the dirt,
stepping softly, leaving paw prints that fade away with the rain.
The creature takes just what it needs from the earth
and nothing more.
When her time comes,
she lies down and dies, leaving her body exposed,
unafraid to be devoured by the vultures
because she knows that her spirit will then fly.

Man walks with feet covered in waterproof boots,
forging a barrier between himself and the earth,
afraid to get dirty.
He stamps through the jungle,
flora and fauna falling at his feet,
bringing down whole ecosystems as he exists.
He makes his harsh mark on this world.
He takes more than what he needs, devours all that he can
because if he is distracted by excess:
fast cars, iPhones, the finest of fashion,
he will not have to face his own wrongdoings.
When man's time comes,
he is buried in the earth,
preventing his spirit from flying free.

Water

A celestial cry from deep in the cosmos calls me to the sea
I make pilgrimage back to the waters of my ancient ancestors

The rippled ringlets distort my reflection on the water's edge
The knife cuts the skin and my legs split the water's clear surface

My blood flows from me like a soprano's soothing swan song
The red dissipates, swallowed by the surrounding blue

I hear the call from the ether, gentle whalesong
Guiding me home, bringing peaceful clarity.

Venom

It warms like the Florida sun soaking into my skin,
swimming faster and faster to feed toxins to all the cells inside.

It burns like the Minnesota cold
creeping up through my veiny tributaries,
climbing peaks and valleys to reach my sacred heart summit.

It calms like my Iowa youth flashing before my eyes—
first kisses, swing sets, Mamma's humming in the kitchen.

Don't tell Mamma that I was trying to die again.

Swallowed

They say the sun will swell up
and engulf this whole planet
someday.

I want to be swallowed up
by pure sunshine.

I want to be free.

About the Author

Charles K. Carter is a queer poet from Iowa who currently lives in Oregon. They share their home with their artist husband and their spoiled pets. He enjoys film, yoga, and live music. Melissa Etheridge is their ultimate obsession. Carter holds an MFA in writing from Lindenwood University. His poems have appeared in numerous literary journals. They are the author of *Read My Lips* from David Robert Books as well as several chapbooks.

Connect on Twitter, Facebook, and Instagram @CKCpoetry

www.CKCpoetry.com

www.ingramcontent.com/pod-product-compliance
Lightning Source LLC
Chambersburg PA
CBHW030913170426
43193CB00009BA/830